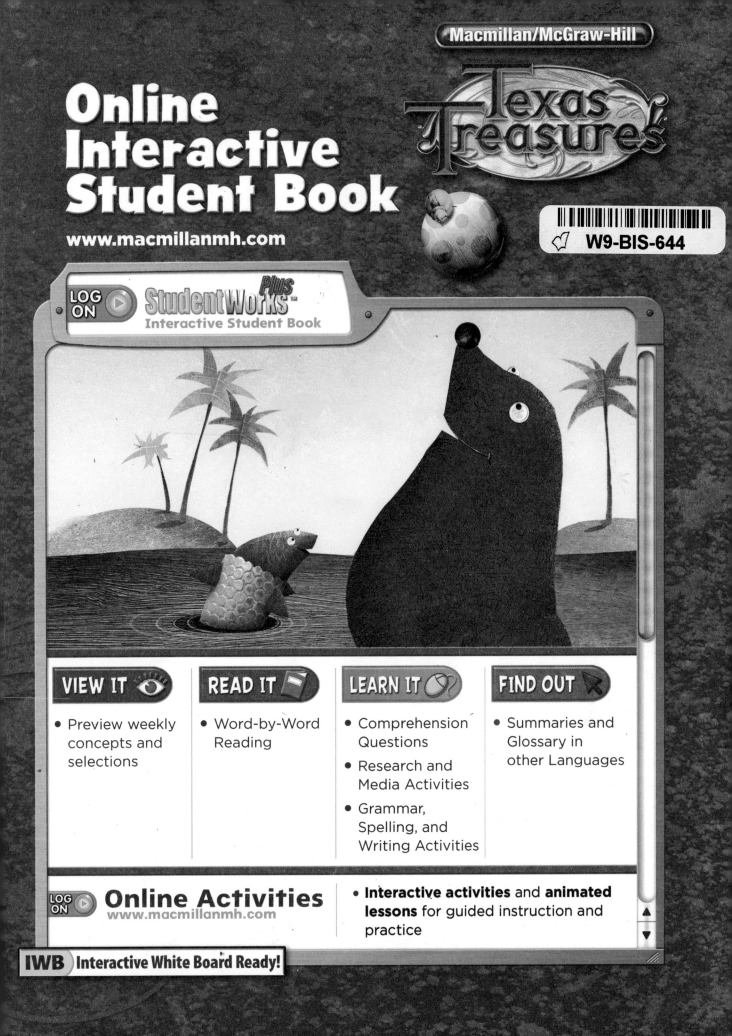

Macmillan/McGraw-Hill

Texas Treasures

Online Interactive Student Book

www.macmillanmh.com

W9-BIS-644

LOG ON ▶ **StudentWorks** *Plus*
Interactive Student Book

VIEW IT 👁

- Preview weekly concepts and selections

READ IT 📖

- Word-by-Word Reading

LEARN IT 🪐

- Comprehension Questions
- Research and Media Activities
- Grammar, Spelling, and Writing Activities

FIND OUT ▶

- Summaries and Glossary in other Languages

LOG ON ▶ **Online Activities**
www.macmillanmh.com

- **Interactive activities** and **animated lessons** for guided instruction and practice

IWB Interactive White Board Ready!

Texas Treasures

A Reading/Language Arts Program

 **Macmillan/McGraw-Hill**

Contributors

Time Magazine, Accelerated Reader

learning through listening

Students with print disabilities may be eligible to obtain an accessible, audio version of the pupil edition of this textbook. Please call Recording for the Blind & Dyslexic at 1-800-221-4792 for complete information.

B

The McGraw·Hill Companies

Macmillan/McGraw-Hill

Published by Macmillan/McGraw-Hill, of McGraw-Hill Education, a division of The McGraw-Hill Companies, Inc., Two Penn Plaza, New York, New York 10121.

Printed in the United States of America

ISBN: 978-0-02-200021-9
MHID: 0-02-200021-6

5 6 7 8 9 DOW 13 12 11 10

Texas Treasures

A Reading/Language Arts Program

Program Authors

Diane August

Donald R. Bear

Janice A. Dole

Jana Echevarria

Douglas Fisher

David Francis

Vicki Gibson

Jan E. Hasbrouck

Scott G. Paris

Timothy Shanahan

Josefina V. Tinajero

Macmillan/McGraw-Hill

Unit 4

Teamwork
Let's Team Up

THEME: Helping the Community

THEME: Better Together

THEME: Animal Teams

Show What You Know • REVIEW

The

Big

Question

How do teams work together?

LOG ON ▶ VIEW IT

Theme Video
Let's Team Up
www.macmillanmh.com

3

How do teams work together?

Have you ever been on a team? What kind of team was it? How did you help? Some people think teams are just for sports. But there are many other kinds of teams. Your family is a kind of team. If you work on a project with a friend, then you two are a team. Even animals can be part of a team! What kinds of teams do you know about?

Research Activities

Think about the teams in the stories you are reading. Pick a story that shows teamwork. Act it out in order. Work as a team.

Keep Track of Ideas

As you read, keep track of different kinds of teams. Use the **Layered Book Foldable** to write down your ideas about how different teams work together.

FOLDABLES®
Study Organizer

What can teams do?

A team can _____.

A team can _____.

A team can _____.

A team can _____.

Digital Learning

LOG ON ▶ **FIND OUT** www.macmillanmh.com

StudentWorks Plus
Interactive Student Book

- **Research Roadmap**
  Follow a step-by-step guide to complete your research project.

Texas Online Resources

- Topic Finder and Other Research Tools
- Videos and Virtual Field Trips
- Photos and Drawings for Presentations
- Related Articles and Web Resources
- Texas Web Site Links

All About TEXAS

Michael Johnson, Athlete

Michael Johnson has been called the world's fastest man. He was crowned world champion nine times and won four Olympic gold medals. At the Olympics he helped to bring the U.S. relay team to victory.

Teammates

What is a team?
What kinds of teams
do you know about?

LOG
ON ▶ VIEW IT

Oral Language Activities
Teammates
www.macmillanmh.com

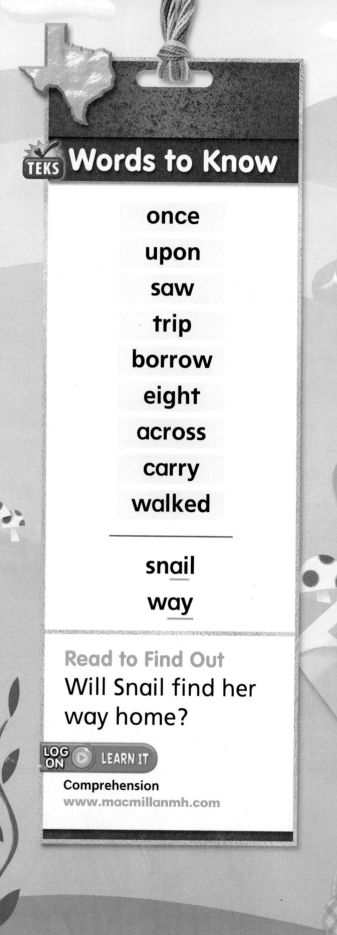

once

upon

saw

trip

borrow

eight

across

carry

walked

---

sn**ai**l

w**ay**

Read to Find Out
Will Snail find her way home?

LOG ON ▶ **LEARN IT**

Comprehension
www.macmillanmh.com

Frog and Snail's Trip

Once upon a time, Frog **saw** a snail. The snail looked sad.

"I was on a **trip** but I lost my way," said Snail.

"I have a map," said Frog.

"Can I **borrow** it?" asked Snail.

"Where is your home?" asked Frog.

"It is past these **eight** hills and **across** that pond," said Snail.

"I will go with you," said Frog. "If you **carry** the map, I will carry the snacks."

So the two new friends **walked** to Snail's home together.

Comprehension

Genre
A Folktale is a story that has been told for many years.

Ask Questions

Make Predictions
Use your Predictions Chart.

What I Predict	What Happens

Read to Find Out
What happens when Drakes Tail goes to see the king?

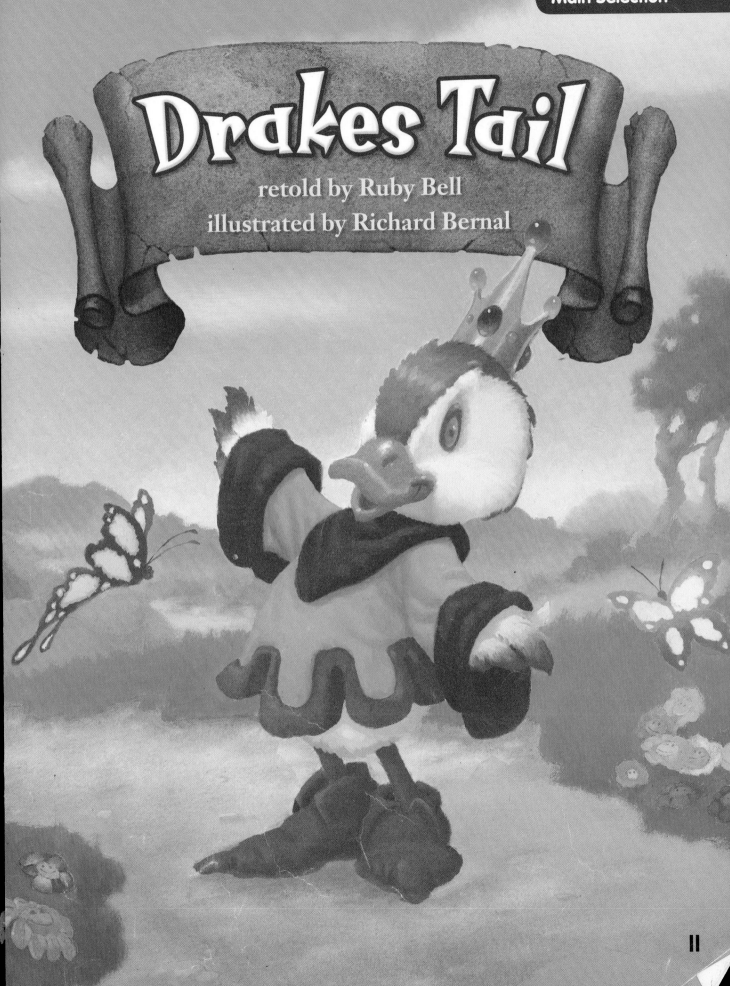

Drakes Tail

retold by Ruby Bell

illustrated by Richard Bernal

Once upon a time, there was a duck
named Drakes Tail.

Drakes Tail was a duck with brains. He
saved all of his money. One day, the king
asked to **borrow** some. Drakes Tail said yes.

Drakes Tail waited for the king to pay him back. But the king did not.

So Drakes Tail set off to see the king.

"Quack! Quack! Quack! Time to get my money back!" he sang.

On his way, Drakes Tail **saw** his friend Fox.

"Fox!" said Drakes Tail, "I am going to the king to get my money back!"

"Take me," said Fox. "I can help!"

"I will," said Drakes Tail. "But it is a long **trip**. You may get tired. Make yourself little and hop in my bag. I will **carry** you."

Fox did as Drakes Tail said.

"Quack! Quack! Quack! Time to get my money back!" sang Drakes Tail.

Then Drakes Tail saw his friend Pond.

"I am going to the king to get my money back," said Drakes Tail.

"May I go with you?" asked Pond.

"Yes," said Drakes Tail. "But it is a long trip. You may get tired. Make yourself little and hop in my bag."

Pond did as Drakes Tail said.

"Quack! Quack! Quack! Time to get my money back!" sang Drakes Tail.

Drakes Tail spotted his friend Hive.

"I am going to the king to get my money back," said Drakes Tail.

Hive wished to come, too. So Hive got little and hopped in Drakes Tail's bag.

Drakes Tail **walked across** the land.

After **eight** days, he made it to the king's palace.

"Quack! Quack! Quack! Can I have my money back?" Drakes Tail asked the king.

But the king had spent it all!

"Stick that duck in the hen pen!" yelled the king.

The hens pecked at Drakes Tail!

"Fox! Fox! I am in bad shape. Come and help me get out of this scrape!" sang Drakes Tail.

Fox hopped out of Drakes Tail's bag. He chased the hens away.

Drakes Tail went back to the king.
"Quack! Quack! Quack! Can I have
my money back?"

"That duck shall make a fine snack!" said
the king. "Put him in a pot!"

"Pond! Pond! I am in a bad spot. Put out the fire that is so hot!" sang Drakes Tail.

Pond gushed out of the bag and put out the fire. Drakes Tail ran.

24

"Catch that duck!" yelled the king.

Drakes Tail sang, "Hive! Hive! Help me please! It is time to send the bees!"

Hive sent its bees to sting the king and his men. They ran and ran.

Drakes Tail sat on the king's throne to rest. Just then, the people of the kingdom came in.

"Drakes Tail is a duck with brains. Let's make him our king!" they said.

Drakes Tail sang, "I will be the king today, if you say my friends can stay!"

From that day on, Drakes Tail ruled the kingdom. He had Fox, Pond, and Hive at his side.

Richard Bernal's Tale

Richard Bernal says, "I have always liked to illustrate old stories like *Drakes Tail*, to help make them seem new. I also love to illustrate birds. I often go to the zoo to take photographs of birds. It was a pleasure to create a little duck like Drakes Tail."

**Other books
by Richard Bernal**

LOG ON ▶ FIND OUT
Illustrator Richard Bernal
www.macmillanmh.com

Illustrator's Purpose

Richard Bernal likes to illustrate old stories. Draw a character from an old story you like. Write about your drawing.

✓ TEKS Comprehension Check

Retell the Story

Use the Retelling Cards
to retell the story in order.

Retelling Cards

Think and Compare

What I Predict	What Happens

1. What does Drakes Tail do when the king does not pay him back?

   Details

2. What happens after Drakes Tail gets to the king's palace?

   Sequence

3. What did you predict would happen when Drakes Tail first saw Hive? What made you predict that?

   Make Predictions

4. How are Drakes Tail and his friends like Frog and Snail in "Frog and Snail's Trip"? Reading Across Texts

Busy As a Bee

Buzz, buzz, buzz! Bees are at home in a hive. They are so busy! All of them have jobs that help the hive.

Bees can make a hive in a tree.

30

Worker bees make wax cups called honeycombs.

Lots of **worker** bees live in a hive. They make **honey**. They help the hive stay clean. They fan the hive with their wings when it gets hot.

Every hive has a **queen** bee. What is her job? She lays eggs.

A hive has drone bees, too. A drone's job is to help the queen make eggs.

A queen bee is with her drones in the hive.

The queen lays eggs inside wax cups.

New bees hatch from these eggs. Worker bees feed them.

As time passes, a hive can get quite big. Buzz, buzz, buzz! A big hive is a busy place!

TEKS Connect and Compare

- How do the captions help you understand the pictures?
- What can you learn from the pictures? Point to the eggs in the photograph on this page.

TEKS *Was* and *Were*

The verbs was and were tell about the past.

Write About Being on a Team

Carlos wrote about being on a kickball team.

We were playing kickball in Pine Park. After I kicked, I ran to all the bases. I was glad I helped the team!

34

Your Turn

Have you ever been on a team or worked with others?

Write about it.

Tell what you did and how you helped.

Grammar and Writing

- Read Carlos's writing.
  Who does the verb were tell about?
  Who does the verb was tell about?
  Point to the special place name.

- Read your writing.
  Did you write about being on a team?
  Did you use was and were correctly?

- Read your writing to a partner.

Family Time

How do people in your family help each other?

LOG ON ▶ VIEW IT

Oral Language Activities
Family Time
www.macmillanmh.com

give

were

says

pretty

splendid

about

write

concentrate

———————

Jean

she

Read to Find Out

How does the girl feel about her big sister?

Comprehension
www.macmillanmh.com

38

When Jean Comes Home

I like it when Jean comes home from school.

I **give** her a big hug. "You **were** away for such a long time!" I say.

"I missed you!" Jean **says**. She gives me a gift. It is a **pretty** doll.

Mom and Dad are glad Jean is back home. "You look **splendid**," they say.

Jean tells us **about** school. She has to read and **write** a lot. She has to **concentrate** to get her work done.

But now Jean is back with us. "Do you want to play?" she asks me.

"Yes!" I say.

Comprehension

Genre
Fiction is a story with made-up characters and events.

TEKS **Ask Questions**
Character and Setting
Use your Character and Setting Chart.

What the Characters Do	Where They Do It

Read to Find Out
What do Gram and James do together?

Gram and Me

by Miriam Cohen

illustrated by Floyd Cooper

Award Winning
Author
and
Illustrator

I like my grandmother a lot.
I call her Gram.
She is so much fun.

Gram takes me fishing.
We sit on the dock.
We wave at the boats.
"Hello!" we call.

Gram helps me ride my bike.
It has two wheels.
"You can do it, James!" she **says**.
"I can ride!" I say.

Gram has a cat named Bean.
Bean feels soft when I pet him.
"Scratch him under his chin," she says.
"Bean likes it!" I say.

Gram and I play chess.
She helps me when we play.
"**Concentrate**, James," she says.
"I win, Gram!" I say.

Gram has a lot of **pretty** flowers.
She lets me **give** them a drink.
"Flowers need a good drink," she says.
"Look! They drank it up," I say.

Gram has a big plum tree.
We like to pick plums.
Gram lifts me so I can reach them.
"I got a ripe one!" I say.

Gram teaches me how to make plum jam.
She adds salt to the pot.
"Just a bit," she says.
"Yum! This jam will taste good!" I say.

"Gram, did you cook when you **were** little?" I ask.

"I helped my mom," says Gram. "We made jam just like you and I do."

"Did you go to school?" I ask.
"Yes, I went to a little school," says Gram.
"My school is big," I say.
"Yes, it is," says Gram.

"I am learning to read and **write** at school,"
I say.
"That is good," says Gram. "I learned to read
and write when I was just your age."
"Gram, can you read me a story?"

"Yes," says Gram. "Do you like cats
and dogs?"
"I like them a lot!" I say.
"This is a story **about** cats and dogs."

I like Gram's story a lot.
"Let's read more," I say.
"Can you read a story to me?" asks Gram.
"I think I can."

"I will read you this story," I say.
"Is it about cats and dogs?" Gram asks.
"No, it is a story about pigs."
"Pigs are good, too," says Gram.

"This is a story about three little pigs," I say.
I read on and on.

At the end, Gram claps and claps.
"What a **splendid** story," she says.
"Gram, you are so much fun," I say.
"So are you," says my Gram.

We Remember Gram

Miriam Cohen says, "I wrote this story about a grandma because I loved mine so much. She told me stories about when she was a girl."

Another book by Miriam Cohen

Floyd Cooper says, "I loved my gram's gingerbread. I start my paintings by spreading gingerbread-colored paint on paper. So, I remember Gram every time I make a painting!"

LOG ON ▶ FIND OUT

Author Miriam Cohen
Illustrator Floyd Cooper
www.macmillanmh.com

Another book by Floyd Cooper

Author's Purpose

Miriam Cohen wrote about her grandma.
Write about a relative who is special to you.

TEKS Comprehension Check

Retell the Story

Use the Retelling Cards to retell the story in order.

Retelling Cards

Think and Compare

What the Characters Do	Where They Do It

1. What does Gram do when James finishes reading? Details

2. What do James and Gram do together? Where do they do it?

   Character and Setting

3. How do James and Gram feel about each other? Point to details that support your answer. Character

4. How are James and the little sister in "When Jean Comes Home" alike?

   Read Across Texts

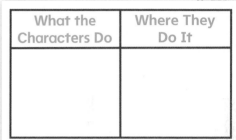

Chinese New Year

Social Studies

Genre
Nonfiction tells about real people, places, and events.

TEKS **Text Feature**
A Numerical List is a series of things written in 1, 2, 3 order.

Content Vocabulary
celebrate
relatives
parade

LOG ON ▶ FIND OUT

Social Studies Celebrations
www.macmillanmh.com

Chinese New Year is a lot of fun. Let's see how kids celebrate it.

Things to Do

1. Make things to eat.

2. Make a costume.

3. Get a flag.

4. Get gifts.

To get set, Ming Lee makes a list.
She has a lot to do!

On the big day, Ming Lee and her mom
and dad go to see **relatives**. They bring
gifts. Kids like Ming Lee get red packets
with money in them. They eat treats
like New Year's cake.

The day ends in a big **parade**. People dress up. They wave big flags. It is such a fun way to start the year!

TEKS **Connect and Compare**

- How do you celebrate the new year?
- How might James and Gram from *Gram and Me* celebrate the new year?

Writing

TEKS *Has* and *Have*

The verbs has and have tell about now.

Write a Letter

Brittany wrote about a garden.

Dear Mom and Dad,

It is so much fun here. Gramps has a garden. Every day we pick vegetables. Then we have salad. I like salad a lot now!

Love,
Brittany

Your Turn

Write a letter to a family member. Write about something you did or would like to do.

Begin your letter with a greeting. End it with a closing.

Grammar and Writing

- Read Brittany's letter.
  Who does the verb has tell about?
  Who does the verb have tell about?
  Point to the greeting and the closing.

- Check your letter.
  Do you use a greeting and a closing?
  Will it make sense to your readers?
  Do you use has and have correctly?

- Read your letter to the family member.

How can we work together to make our community better?

Oral Language Activities
Helping the Community
www.macmillanmh.com

Helping the Community

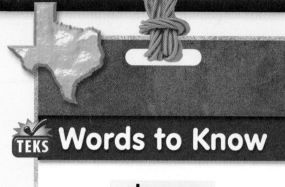

change
better
ripe
difficult
move
buy
_____

gr<u>o</u>w
g<u>o</u>

Picking Peaches

We have peach trees. When the peaches are little, they are not good. But then they **change**. They taste much **better** when they grow.

68

When the peaches are **ripe** it is time to pick them. We have a **difficult** job. We work as a team. We **move** from tree to tree, picking as we go.

The next time you **buy** a peach, think about where it came from. Think about the people who picked that peach.

César Chávez

César Chávez was a great man. In his life he helped a lot of people. He helped people who picked crops the most.

70

Farmers grow crops, such as grapes and peaches.

When the crops are **ripe**, they need to be picked. Then crop pickers come to pick the crops.

For a long time, these crop pickers had a **difficult** life. They picked crops in the hot sun all day. The farmers did not pay them much.

When there were no crops left,
the pickers had to **move**.

They had many homes each year.
But the homes were not good.
The crop pickers lived in shacks.

César Chávez did not like this. He wanted the crop pickers to have a **better** life. He felt that if people worked together, things could **change**.

Grapes were one of the biggest crops. César Chávez told the crop pickers not to pick grapes. He told people not to **buy** grapes.

The grapes began to rot.
The farmers did not like this.

The crop pickers marched with César Chávez. They spoke to the farmers. They asked for more pay. They asked for better homes.

◀ César Chávez stands with grape pickers.

It took a long time, but the farmers did make changes.

Today crop pickers have a better life. They get more pay. They live in better homes. They thank César Chávez, who helped them work together.

Comprehension Check

Tell What You Learned

What did you learn about César Chávez?

Think and Compare

1. Who did César Chávez help the most?
   Retell

2. What was it like for the crop pickers before César Chávez helped them? How did their lives change? Retell

3. Why do you think César Chávez told people not to buy grapes? Draw Conclusions

4. What might César Chávez have said to the peach pickers in "Picking Peaches"?
   Reading Across Texts

Answering Questions
Sometimes the answer is on the page. Sometimes it is not. You must look for clues.

Food Trains

Where do the crops you eat come from? Some food you eat may be grown hundreds of miles away!

How can crops grown so far away stay fresh? A long time ago they couldn't. But then trains were made. Crops could go fast in these trains. Cold cars kept the crops cold. That helped keep them fresh.

Today crops can go in trucks and on planes. Now we can eat a peach, bean, or grape grown a long way away.

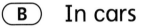

DIRECTIONS
Answer the questions.

1 How can crops go across the country today?

    (A)   In trucks

    (B)   In cars

    (C)   On horses

2 Cold train cars helped the crops —

    (A)   grow more

    (B)   stay fresh

    (C)   change color

3 Which kinds of food is the story about?

    (A)   Bread and eggs

    (B)   Fruits and vegetables

    (C)   Cheese and milk

READ TOGETHER

Write About a Person You Admire

Crystal wrote about a lifeguard.

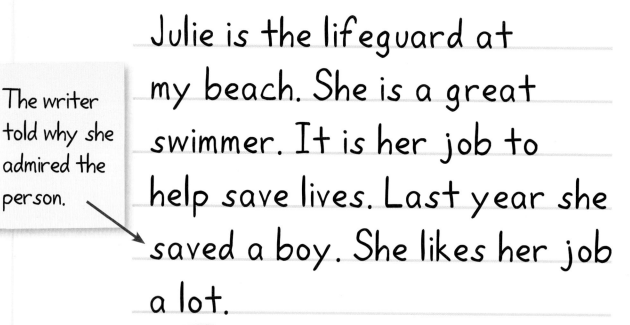

The writer told why she admired the person.

Julie is the lifeguard at my beach. She is a great swimmer. It is her job to help save lives. Last year she saved a boy. She likes her job a lot.

Write to a Prompt

Think of a person you admire. It could be a person you know or have heard about.

Write a report telling about the person you admire.

Writing Hints

 Tell why the person you admire is special.

 Write clearly so that readers will understand you.

☑ Check your report for mistakes.

Better Together

83

ball
perhaps
head
should
shout
meadow
never

_____

fly
high

Read to Find Out

What helps Little Cub hit the ball?

LOG ON ▶ **LEARN IT**

Comprehension
www.macmillanmh.com

See the Ball Fly!

Little Cub is up at bat. He swings, but he misses the **ball**.

He shakes his **head**.

"**Perhaps** I **should** not be at bat," he thinks.

"You can do it, Little Cub!" **shout** his teammates.

On his next try, Little Cub hits the ball. He sees it fly high over the **meadow**.

"I've **never** hit a ball that well!" he thinks. Then he runs to each base.

Genre

A **Fantasy** is a made-up story that could not really happen.

Visualize

Plot

Use your Plot Chart.

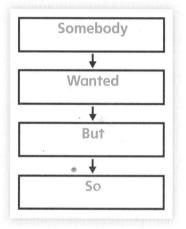

Somebody

↓

Wanted

↓

But

↓

So

Read to Find Out

How will Frog and Toad fly the kite?

The Kite

from
Days with Frog and Toad

by Arnold Lobel

Frog and Toad went out

to fly a kite.

They went to

a large **meadow**

where the wind was strong.

"Our kite will fly up and up,"

said Frog.

"It will fly all the way up

to the top of the sky."

"Toad," said Frog,

"I will hold the **ball** of string.

You hold the kite and run."

Toad ran across the meadow.

He ran as fast as his short legs
could carry him.

The kite went up in the air.

It fell to the ground with a bump.

Toad heard laughter.

Three robins were sitting in a bush.

"That kite will not fly,"
said the robins.
"You may as well give up."

Toad ran back to Frog.
"Frog," said Toad,
"this kite will not fly.
I give up."

"We must make a second try,"
said Frog.

"Wave the kite over your **head**.
Perhaps that will make it fly."

Toad ran back across the meadow.

He waved the kite over his head.

The kite went up in the air

and then fell down with a thud.

"What a joke!" said the robins.

"That kite will **never**

get off the ground."

Toad ran back to Frog.

"This kite is a joke," he said.

"It will never get off the ground."

"We have to make
a third try," said Frog.

"Wave the kite over your head
and jump up and down.

Perhaps that will make it fly."

Toad ran across

the meadow again.

He waved the kite

over his head.

He jumped up and down.

The kite went up in the air

and crashed down into the grass.

"That kite is junk,"

said the robins.

"Throw it away and go home."

Toad ran back to Frog.

"This kite is junk," he said.

"I think we **should**

throw it away and go home."

"Toad," said Frog,

"we need one more try.

Wave the kite over your head.

Jump up and down

and **shout** UP KITE UP."

Toad ran across the meadow.

He waved the kite over his head.

He jumped up and down.

He shouted, "UP KITE UP!"

The kite flew into the air.

It climbed higher and higher.

"We did it!" cried Toad.

"Yes," said Frog.

"If a running try

did not work,

and a running and waving try

did not work,

and a running, waving,

and jumping try

did not work,

I knew that

a running, waving, jumping,

and shouting try

just had to work."

The robins flew out of the bush.

But they could not fly

as high as the kite.

Frog and Toad sat

and watched their kite.

It seemed to be flying

way up at the top of the sky.

Arnold Lobel's Story

Arnold Lobel was often sick and missed many days of school when he was young. When he went back to school, he made friends by telling stories and drawing pictures. Many years later, Lobel's children liked to catch frogs and toads. Lobel loved the animals and wrote about them in his Frog and Toad stories.

Other books by Arnold Lobel

LOG ON ▶ FIND OUT

Author Arnold Lobel
www.macmillanmh.com

Author's Purpose

Arnold Lobel wanted to write about good friends. Write about your friend. Tell how you help each other.

TEKS Comprehension Check

Retell the Story

Use the Retelling Cards
to retell the story in order.

Retelling Cards

Think and Compare

1. Who is this story about?

   Details

2. What do the robins tell Toad
   about the kite?   Retell

3. What problem do Frog and
   Toad have? How do they
   solve it?   Plot

4. What do Little Cub in "See the Ball Fly!"
   and Frog and Toad have in common?

   Read Across Texts

Somebody
↓
Wanted
↓
But
↓
So

The Wright Brothers

Wilbur and Orville Wright were brothers. People called them Will and Orv.

Will and Orv both liked fixing things.
They liked to ride things, too.

Will and Orv liked bikes a lot. They had
a bike shop.

Will and Orv had wheels. But they wanted wings. They wanted to fly.

In those days long ago, there were no planes. So Will and Orv got to work. First they made a glider. A glider is like a kite that a person can ride on.

Will and Orv liked the glider. But they wanted it to do more. They saw birds use their wings and tails to help them go up and down and turn.

Will and Orv got to work. They **invented** a **machine**. It was the first **airplane**. The plane had propellers and an engine. These helped the plane move like a bird.

On a cold day in 1903, Will and Orv tried the plane. It went up! It stayed up for 12 seconds. That is not a lot, but it showed that the plane worked!

This is how we can get places today. We can go on land, by water, and high up in the sky.

Thanks to Wilbur and Orville Wright, we can fly!

How We Get Places

Land	Sea	Air
car	sailboat	plane
train	ship	helicopter

TEKS **Connect and Compare**

- How did the Wright brothers act like a team?
- How can we travel by land? What is shown on the chart? How else can we travel by land?

Writing

TEKS **See and *Saw***

The verb *see* tells about now. The verb *saw* tells about the past.

Write a Story

Skye wrote about animal friends.

Jake, the mouse, was hungry.

"I saw a nut on the tree

yesterday," he said.

"I can *see* it now!" said a little bird.

"I will get it for you."

"Thank you!" said Jake.

Your Turn

Write a made-up story about friends.

Think about who your friends are.

Tell how they could help
each other.

Include a beginning,
a middle, and an end.

Grammar and Writing

- Read Skye's story.
  Retell the beginning, middle, and end.
  Find the words see and saw.
  Which tells about now? Which tells about
  the past?

- Check your story.
  Is there a beginning, middle and end?
  Did you use see and saw correctly?

- Read your story to a partner.

Animal Teams

Talk About It

Do you think animals can help each other? How?

Oral Language Activities
Animal Teams
www.macmillanmh.com

III

or

danger

because

also

other

until

beautiful

blue

---

tiny

yummy

Read to Find Out

Why do fish swim together in a school?

LOG ON ▶ **LEARN IT**

Comprehension

www.macmillanmh.com

A School of Fish

Some fish swim together in a school. What is a school of fish? It is many big **or** tiny fish swimming in a bunch.

A school of fish works like a team. Many fish swimming together can see **danger** better than a fish by itself can. The fish swim in a school **because** they will be safer.

Fish in schools **also** can find more to eat. Why? It's because many, many fish are looking at the same time. The fish look for plants and **other** yummy things. They look **until** they see things they like eating. So, in a lake or the **beautiful blue** sea, it helps fish to be in school!

113

Genre
Nonfiction gives information about a topic.

Visualize
Retell

Use your Retelling Chart.

Retell

Read to Find Out
How do animals act as teams?

114

Animal Teams

By Rachel Mann

Can a little bird help a big giraffe?
Can a shrimp help a fish?

Yes, they can!

These might seem like funny friends. But many kinds of animals work together in teams. These animals help each **other** in lots of ways. Let's find out how.

Some birds live
on the backs of
big animals. Why
do the animals
let the birds stay?
The birds help.
They eat bugs off
the animals' skin.

The big animals help the little birds, too. The birds are safe on top of these big pals. And they are happy **because** they have lots of yummy bugs to eat!

The goby fish and the blind shrimp make a good team.

The shrimp can't see, so the goby helps. The goby looks out for **danger**, and the shrimp stays close. When the goby flicks its tail, it means that it is time to hide.

The shrimp helps the goby, too. It has a hole to hide in. It lets the goby hide there, too. The shrimp and the goby hide **until** it is safe to go out.

Zebras and wildebeests live on the hot, sunny plains. They both like to graze on grass all day.

These animals are seen together a lot. Why?

They stay together because they can help each other find fresh grass to eat.

They **also** help each other stay safe. If a zebra **or** a wildebeest spots danger, it runs. This tells the rest to run, too.

Many fish want to eat the little clown fish. It needs a safe home. So it lives in a sea anemone.

The clown fish is safe because most fish stay away. Why? The sea anemone stings! But the clown fish can not feel its sting.

The clown fish helps its buddy, too. It swims in and out, in and out. It chases away big fish that might hurt its pal.

A caterpillar needs to be safe so that it can grow.

Who will help? Ants will! They find the caterpillar and take it to a safe place.

Why do ants do this?

The caterpillar has a sweet liquid on its skin. The ants like the taste.

Soon the caterpillar will be a **beautiful blue** butterfly.

When a little cleaner fish is hungry, it looks for bigger fish to clean. Why? It gets a free meal when it cleans.

A cleaner fish eats the pests off of other fish.

The fish want to be cleaned. They line up and wait for the cleaner fish to get to them.

One is big, and one is little.
But the two are friends.

When animals team up, they do what
is best for both of them.

Join Rachel Mann's Team

Rachel Mann loves learning about animals, especially animals who act in unexpected ways. She really enjoyed researching and writing *Animal Teams* because she learned that animals help and need each other just as people do.

LOG ON ▶ FIND OUT

Author Rachel Mann
www.macmillanmh.com

TEKS Author's Purpose

Rachel Mann wanted to write about animals who do interesting things. Write about an animal that does something you find interesting.

Comprehension Check

Retell the Selection

Use the Retelling Cards
to retell the selection in order.

Retelling Cards

Think and Compare

1. How does the goby fish help the blind shrimp? Details

2. How can little animals help a bigger animal? Retell

3. What did you learn about animals from this selection? What is it mainly about?

   Main Idea and Details

4. How are the animals in *Animal Teams* like the fish in "A School of Fish"?

   Read Across Texts

Retell

133

Poetry

Genre

Poetry helps readers look at things they see every day in new ways.

TEKS Literary Elements

Repetition is the way words in a poem are used more than once.

Rhythm Poems are written so that the words have a certain beat, or rhythm, when you say them aloud.

LOG ON ▶ **FIND OUT**

Poetry Animal Poems
www.macmillanmh.com

READ TOGETHER

Where?

by Charlotte Zolotow

I look up into the sky
and see the birds
like black arrows
flying high.
Where they come from where they go
Only they really know
flying flying flying by
in the blueness of the sky.

TEKS Connect and Compare

- How are the birds in the poem acting like the animals in *Animal Teams*?
- What words and word parts do you emphasize when saying the poem aloud?

135

TEKS Adverbs

Adverbs can tell when something happened.

Write About an Animal Team

Sam wrote about animals from *Animal Teams*.

The shrimp digs a hole. Next, the goby goes in. That way the goby stays safe. The goby helps the shrimp too. It swims with the shrimp so no one will hurt it.

Your Turn

Think of an animal team you know or have read about.

Write about the animals.

Tell how they work together.

Grammar and Writing

- Read Sam's report.
  Find the adverb that tells when.
  Find the comma. Point to the capital letter that begins each sentence.

- Check your report.
  Do you tell clearly how each animal helps?
  Do you use adverbs correctly?

- Read your report to a partner.

TEKS

Review

Retell
Character and Setting
Labels
Captions
Context Clues

Ray and His Bones

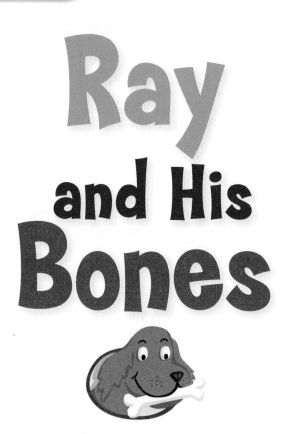

My dog Ray loves bones. One day when it snowed, Mom gave Ray a bone. He was thrilled and wagged his tail.

Next Ray held the bone in his teeth. He ran to the backyard. He dug a hole. He dropped in the bone and piled on snow.

All winter, Ray buried his bones in the snow. He buried bones from our meals. He buried bones from our friends' meals. In all, Ray buried nine bones!

How did we know Ray buried nine bones? That's easy. When the snow melted, we could see each bone!

As Tall as the Trees

Giraffes are the tallest mammals. Long necks and legs help make them so tall. They have manes and tiny horns.

Giraffes can reach high with those long necks. They can eat the leaves at the tops of trees.

Giraffes get food and water from leaves.

A male giraffe is called a bull.
A bull can be nineteen feet tall.
A female giraffe is called a cow.
A cow can grow to be sixteen feet.
A baby giraffe is called a calf.
It can be as big as six feet at birth.

Read the labels that name some parts of a giraffe. Name more parts that you see.

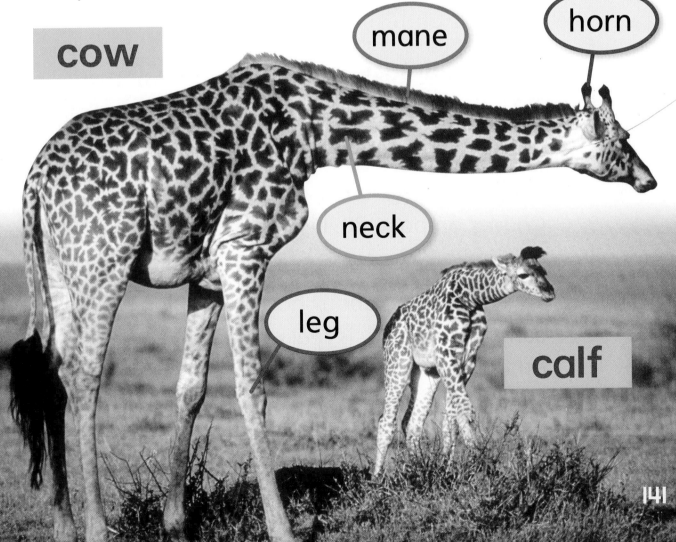

cow

mane

horn

neck

leg

calf

Word Study

Compound Words

- Read the compound words below. Find the two smaller words in each.

  popcorn   sailboat   football   sunrise

- Draw pictures that show each smaller word. Talk about how the smaller words help you understand the larger word.

Comprehension

Real and Fantasy Heroes

- César Chávez and Drakes Tail both acted bravely and helped others.

- Reread *Drakes Tail* on page 10 and *César Chávez* on page 70. List ways that they each act like heroes.

- Talk in a group about how you can tell one story is real and the other is a fantasy.

Writing

Story Time!

- Write a story about teamwork.

- Think of characters for your story. Will they be people or animals?

- Think of a problem your characters have. This will be in the beginning of your story.

- Think of how they can try to solve the problem. This will be in the middle of your story.

- Think of how the problem is solved. This will be at the end of your story.

- Share your story with the class!

Glossary

What Is a Glossary?

A glossary can help you find the meanings of words. The words are listed in alphabetical order. You can look up a word and read it in a sentence. Sometimes there is a picture.

carry

difficult

Sample Entry

Letter

B b

Main Entry

ball

Sentence

This **ball** is fun at the beach.

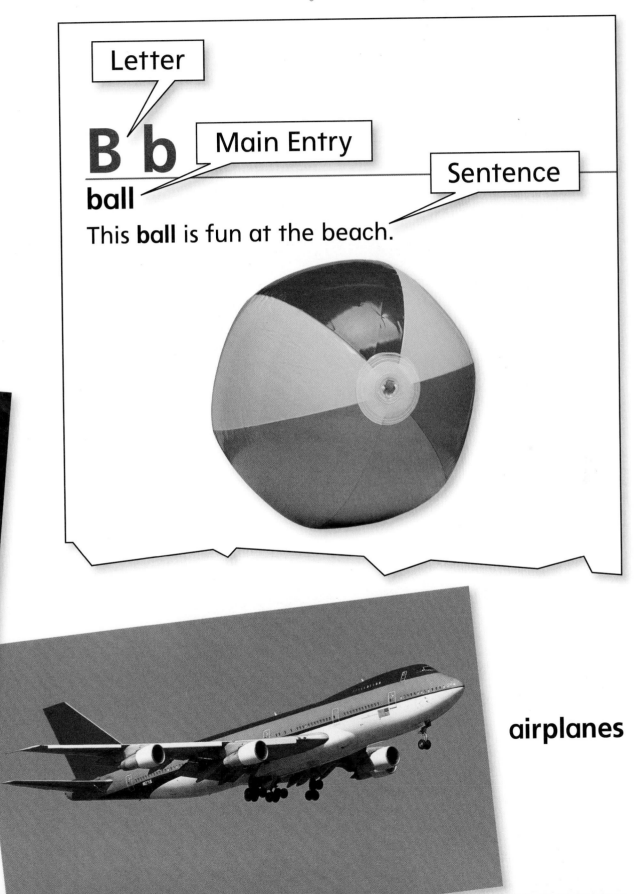

airplanes

Aa

about

Ms. Dunne told us a story **about** ducks.

across

Mike walked **across** the bridge.

airplanes

Airplanes can go very fast.

also

I like to bake bread and **also** eat it.

Bb

ball

This **ball** is fun
at the beach.

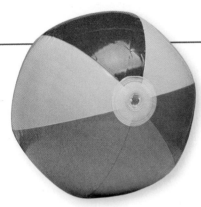

beautiful

Mary's painting is **beautiful**.

because

It's time to leave **because** the movie is over.

better

Greg likes apples **better** than pears.

blue

The sky looks so **blue** today.

borrow

I **borrow** books from the library.

buy

If you **buy** shoes, make sure they fit.

Cc

carry

This animal can **carry** her baby on her back.

celebrate

We **celebrate** Thanksgiving with a big family dinner.

change

The traffic light will soon **change** from red to green.

concentrate

I need to **concentrate** when I read.

Dd

danger

When the cat wakes up, the mouse will be in **danger**.

difficult

It's **difficult** to stand like this.

Ee

eight

When will you become **eight** years old?

Gg

give

It is nice to **give** gifts.

Hh

head

Keisha wears a helmet to protect her **head**.

honey

Honey is sweet and sticky.

Ii

invent

I wish I could **invent** a robot to make my bed.

Mm

machine

A **machine** can help sew clothes.

meadow

The **meadow** is full of flowers.

move

If I **move**, so does my shadow.

Nn

never

Ruby **never** goes to sleep without a story.

Oo

once

Once dinosaurs walked the earth.

or

Is the kitten bigger **or** smaller than the dog?

other

Sarah ran and the **other** kids walked.

Pp

parade

Everyone dressed up for the **parade**.

perhaps

Perhaps the sun will come out later.

pretty

The fireworks were very **pretty**.

Qq

queen

The **queen** wore a golden crown.

Rr

relatives

Aunt Sally and Uncle Gene are my favorite **relatives**.

ripe

If the peaches are **ripe**, we'll pick them.

Ss

saw

We **saw** three frogs in the pond.

says

My sister **says** she will be late.

should

You **should** eat a good lunch.

shout

I **shout** when I'm happy.

splendid

What a **splendid** day for a picnic!

Tt

trip

We had a great time on our camping **trip**.

Uu

until

Don't run **until** you hear the starting bell.

upon

My grandfather rested his head **upon** the pillow.

Ww

walked

We **walked** to school today.

were

What grade **were** you in last year?

worker

Worker bees build the hive.

write

I **write** with a pencil.

Acknowledgments

The publisher gratefully acknowledges permission to reprint the following copyrighted material:

"The Kite" from *Days with Frog and Toad* by Arnold Lobel. Text and illustrations copyright © 1979 by Arnold Lobel. Reprinted by permission of Harper & Row Publishers, Inc.

"Where?" from *Seasons: A Book of Poems* by Charlotte Zolotow. Text copyright © 2002 by Charlotte Zolotow. Reprinted by permission of HarperCollins.

Book Cover, FROG AND TOAD ARE FRIENDS by Arnold Lobel. Copyright © 1970 by Arnold Lobel. Reprinted by permission of HarperCollins Publishers.

Book Cover, GRANDPA'S FACE by Eloise Greenfield, illustrated by Floyd Cooper. Text copyright © 1996 by Eloise Greenfield. Illustrations copyright © 1996 by Floyd Cooper. Reprinted by permission of Penguin Putnam Books for Young Readers.

Book Cover, OWL AT HOME by Arnold Lobel. Copyright © 1975 by Arnold Lobel. Reprinted by permission of HarperCollins Children's Books, a division of HarperCollins Publishers.

Book Cover, WHEN WILL I READ? by Miriam Cohen, illustrated by Lillian Hoban. Text copyright © 1977 by Miriam Cohen. Illustrations Copyright © 1977 by Lillian Hoban. Reprinted by permission of Greenwillow Books.

ILLUSTRATIONS

Cover Illustration: Pablo Bernasconi

8–9: Sheree Boyd. 10–29: Richard Bernal. 34: Daniel DelValle. 38–39: Patrice Barton. 40–59: Floyd Cooper. 64: Daniel DelValle. 80: Mindy Pierce. 84–85: Jamie Smith. 86–101: Arnold Lobel. 108–109: Ken Bowser. 134–135: Holly Hannon. 138–139: Jannie Ho.

PHOTOGRAPHY

All photographs are by Ken Cavanagh or Ken Karp for Macmillan/McGraw Hill (MMH) except as noted below.

iv: Roy Botterell/Corbis. v: (tl) Larry Bones/AGE Fotostock; (bl) Dana Hursey/Masterfile. 2–3: Roy Botterell/Corbis. 4: Blend/Punchstock. 4–5: imagebroker/Alamy. 5: Mike Powell/Allsport/Getty Images. 6–7: Jim Cummins/Getty Images. 28: Courtesy of Richard Bernall. 30: Robert C. Hermes/Photo Researchers. 31: (t) Ted Horowitz/Corbis; (cl) Jan Rietz/Getty Images. 32: John B Free/Nature Picture Library. 33: Papilio/Alamy. 34: Artiga/Masterfile. 35: Eyewire/PunchStock. 36–37: Walter Hodges/Getty Images. 58: (tr) Courtesy of Miriam Cohen; (cl) Courtesy of Floyd Cooper. 60: A.Ramey/Photo Edit. 61: (t) Laura Dwight/Omni-Photo Communications; (b) Brand X Pictures/Picture Quest/Jupiter Images. 62: (t) Lawrence Migdale/Photo Researchers; (cl) Michael Newman/Photo Edit; (cr) Phil Schermeister/Corbis. 63: (t) Ted Streshinsky/Corbis; (cr) Nik Wheeler/Corbis. 64: Juice Images/Alamy. 65: Photodisc/Alamy. 66–67: Larry Bones/AGE fotostock. 68: Mark Thomas/Foodpix/Jupiter Images. 69: Jeff Greenberg/Photo Edit. 70: CSU Archives/Everett Collection. 71: Jupiter Images/Agence Images/Alamy. 72: AP Images. 73: Wisconsin Historical Society/Everett Collection. 74: Jason Laure/The Image Works. 75: AP Photo/Barry Sweet. 76: Arthur Schatz/Time Life Pictures/Getty Images. 78: Jeff Greenburg/The Image Works. 80: Corbis/Punchstock. 81: (b) Bet Noire/Shutterstock; (br & tr) C Squared Studios/Getty Images. 82–83: imagel00/Alamy. 100: Courtesy of Arnold Lobel. 102–103: Underwood & Underwood/Corbis; (bkgd) Stockbyte/Getty Images. 104: Corbis. 104–105: Stockbyte/Getty Images. 105: National Archives/Handout/Getty Images. 106: Corbis. 106–107: Stockbyte/Getty Images. 107: (tl, tc, tr) Photodisc/Getty Images; (bl, br) Digital Vision/Getty Images; (bc) PhotoLink/Getty Images. 108: Darren Greenwood/Alamy. 110–111: Tui de Roy/Minden Pictures. 112–113: Fred Bavendam/Minden Pictures. 114–115: Dana Hursey/Masterfile. 116: Photodisc/Punchstock. 117: Georgette Douwma/Photo Researchers. 118–119: Tony Heald/Nature Picture Library. 120–121: Images&Stories/Alamy. 121: Gary Bell/Oceanwideimages.com. 122–123: Karen Tweedy-Holmes/Corbis. 123: Digital Vision/PunchStock. 124: Fred Bavendam/Minden Pictures. 124–125: Stuart Westmorland/Corbis. 126: Arco Images/Alamy. 126–127: Valerie Giles/Photo Researchers. 127: Rick & Nora Bowers/Alamy. 128: Carl Roessler/Animals Animals. 128–129: Fred Bavendam/Minden Pictures. 130–131: Gerard Lacz/Peter Arnold, Inc.. 132: (tr) Courtesy of Julia Smith; (bcl) Rick & Nora Bowers/Alamy. 133: (br) Photodisc/Punchstock; (bl) Karen Tweedy-Holmes/Corbis. 136: Iconica/Getty Images. 137: G.K. & Vicki Hart/Getty Images. 140: Anup Shah/Getty Images. 141: Bigit Koch/Animals Animals. 143: C Squared Studios/Getty Images. 144: (cr) Gary Bell/Zefa/Corbis; (bl) Ken Cavanagh/Macmillan McGraw-Hill. 145: (b) imageshop/Zefa/Alamy; (t) Stockbyte/Punchstock. 146: (t) BananaStock/Alamy; (b) imageshop/Zefa/Alamy. 147: (t) Stockbyte/Punchstock; (b) William Manning/Corbis. 148: (t) Gary Bell/Zefa/Corbis; (b) Paul Barton/Corbis. 149: Ken Cavanagh/Macmillan McGraw-Hill. 150: (t) David Schmidt/Masterfile; (b) Rommel/Masterfile. 151: (t) Digital Vision/Punchstock; (b) Tetra Images/Punchstock. 152: (t) Paul Freytag/Zefa/Corbis; (b) Masterfile Royalty-Free. 153: (t) Helga Lade/Peter Arnold, Inc.; (b) LHB Photo/Alamy. 154: Dynamic Graphics Group/Creatas/Alamy. 155: Corbis. 156: Banana Stock/AGE Fotostock. 157: (t) Masterfile Royalty-Free; (b) LWA-Sharie Kennedy/Corbis.